TALES OF MELRIC THE MAGICIAN

TALES OF MELRIC THE MAGICIAN

DAVID McKEE

TREASURE PRESS

First published in Great Britain in four separate volumes by
Blackie and Son Limited

This edition published in 1991 by
Treasure Press
Michelin House
81 Fulham Road
London SW3 6RB

ISBN 1-85051-626-X

Printed in Czechoslovakia

50775

CONTENTS

The Magician and the Sorcerer

Melric, the magician, and the king had been arguing for weeks. The king wanted Melric to make him as powerful as the famous kings he had been reading about.

"More power," he shouted at Melric. "I want to be known far and wide."

"You're powerful enough," said Melric. "More power will never make you happier. But you'll soon be known far and wide for your voice. That's powerful enough."

"You're useless," the king would grumble. "You won't even do what I command."

And so it went on night after night.

One morning Melric went to see the king and was surprised to see a feast being prepared.

"I have had a message that a sorcerer called Sondrak is coming to visit the palace," said the king. "Who is he?"

"I don't know," said Melric. "I've never heard of him. Perhaps he isn't a real sorcerer at all."

"And perhaps he is," said the king. "Perhaps he's friendlier than some magicians I know, and perhaps he's willing to make a nice little king just a teeny weeny bit more powerful. Anyway, we're giving a feast in his honour, so there."

Melric wanted to know more about this sorcerer and decided to ask his sister, Mertel the witch. With the help of a travelling spell Melric was soon in her cave enjoying a cup of her special brew. Mertel knew most people who had anything to do with magic but she had never heard of Sondrak.

"He could be someone pretending to be a sorcerer," she said. "We can soon find out with this."

She gave Melric a small box of powder. "Sprinkle some on his food. If he really can work magic you will see a light above his head, an orange light for good magic and a blue light for evil. Try some yourself," she added and sprinkled some powder on Melric's seed cake.

Melric bit the cake and looked in the mirror. "I can work good magic," he murmured as he saw the orange light. "I should hope so," laughed Mertel. "What did you expect?" Then as Melric was getting ready to leave she brought a bird out from the back of the cave.

"This is Krik," she said. "Take him, and if you need help send him to Kra, the wise man who lives at the top of the mountain." The two arrived back at the palace just as a messenger came to tell Melric that the feast was about to begin. Sondrak had arrived.

When Melric reached the feasting room the king introduced him to Sondrak who didn't seem very pleased.

"H'm. I see," he said. "What have we here? *A magician.*" Melric sat in his usual place to the right of the king. The feast began and Melric waited for his chance. It came when the king was pointing out something of interest to Sondrak. While they looked the other way Melric slipped some powder on the sorcerer's food. Sondrak took a large mouthful. A light appeared above his head. So he really could work magic. But the colour of the light was . . . BLUE! Sondrak was up to no good.

During the meal the king asked Sondrak what he thought of a magician who refused to make his king more powerful.

"A magician's job is to do what his king asks," said Sondrak.

"For that, my dear Sondrak, I offer you the seat at my right hand," said the king.

"A magician's job is to help the king and that doesn't mean giving him all he asks for willy-nilly," murmured Melric as he changed places with Sondrak. Then he whispered to Krik, "I think Sondrak will be after my job soon, too. You'd better find out what Kra knows of this sorcerer." So Krik left by the nearest window to fly with a fast furious flap to Kra's mountain.

Kra usually protected his mountain with magic to stop visitors from dropping in, but Krik was able to fly straight to a rock beside Kra. "I was expecting you," explained the wise man. "Now about Sondrak. . ." Kra knew everything. He knew why Krik was there even before the bird had a chance to speak. "Sondrak is a wicked sorcerer looking for a land to rule. He wants to take Melric's place. He will pretend to help the king but instead he will *rule* the king and his kingdom."

"Will you help Melric?" Krik asked.

"If Melric is to win his contest with Sondrak then he must do it by himself," said Kra. "But give him this advice. He must not forget the power of laughter."

It was obvious that Kra had no more to say, so Krik flew back to the palace. The feast was over and nearly everyone had gone to bed, glad to have a peaceful night without the king shouting at Melric. But Melric was still waiting up for Krik and he listened eagerly to what Kra had to say. "The power of laughter," said the magician when Krik had finished. "I don't know anything about the power of laughter but I do like the sound of it." Then, still puzzling over Kra's words and wondering what Sondrak would do next, Melric fell asleep.

The next morning Melric was woken by noise outside his window. He looked out and saw Sondrak performing tricks in front of a crowd. Near Melric the king was also watching. When Sondrak had everyone's attention he set out to show just how powerful he was. "I can destroy," he said, and a flash from his hand crumbled a house into ruins. "And I can build," he shouted. Another flash put the house back as it had been. The crowd gasped in amazement.

Then Sondrak ordered six archers to shoot at him. The archers took careful aim and fired their arrows. They flew straight towards the sorcerer but seemed to bounce off an invisible wall in front of him.

"Nothing hurts me," shouted Sondrak. He pointed one hand at the ground and a fire roared up. Then he pointed at the sky and rain poured down, putting out the fire.

"See what power I have," he shouted. "Think how great I could make your king. What could anyone do against me? Especially you, magician?"

Melric looked at Sondrak standing on the edge of a puddle left by the rain and remembered Kra's words. He smiled and pointed at the puddle. The water turned to ice beneath Sondrak's feet. At once Sondrak started to slip and slide and after flying through the air ended on the ground. The crowd roared with laughter.

"STOP LAUGHING," screamed Sondrak who above all else could not bear the sound of laughter. He tried to get up, but his slipping and sliding antics made him look more than ever like a clown. How the crowd laughed.

Sondrak went to put his hands over his ears and his feet shot from under him. Melric pointed again making the ice turn back into the dirty puddle just as Sondrak was landing. SPLASH! Up got a very wet and muddy sorcerer. "Don't laugh," he howled. "You were supposed to fear me. I was going to rule you and your king." His evil plan was out, but everyone just laughed and laughed.

At last Sondrak crept away. "I'm going," he snarled at Melric. "But you haven't heard the last of me."

The king smiled. He suddenly felt much happier.

"You're right, Melric," he said. "I don't need more power." Then he ordered another feast, this time in *Melric's* honour. Melric was pleased that everything had worked out so well but he couldn't help wondering if he would be troubled by Sondrak again.

The Magician and the Balloon

Melric, the magician, was working in his ordinary non-magic workshop when the king and his pet troon came to see what he was doing. "Why do you need a workshop, Melric?" the king asked. "You can make anything by magic."

"Sometimes," Melric replied, "it's more fun to make things yourself."

"Well, what have you been making?" the king asked. "A balloon which can carry me from place to place," Melric replied.

"But you can go anywhere by magic," the king said.

"Sometimes," said Melric, "it's more fun to travel than to arrive." And as the balloon was finished he offered to take the king for a ride.

A magic spell soon had them and the balloon on the roof. "I'm glad you don't think it's fun for us to lift heavy things," smiled the king as they climbed into the basket under the balloon. When they were ready Melric let the balloon just drift off the roof.

As they passed over the countryside the king became very excited. He could see for miles and the people looked like ants. When they travelled over the wood where Melric's sister Mertel, the witch, lived, she flew up on her broomstick to meet them. Melric introduced her to the king but Mertel couldn't stay for long as she had a seed cake in the oven.

Gradually the king became more serious. "Look how close together those houses are," he said. "Look how bendy that road is. It would be much better straight." So for the rest of the trip he kept saying things like, "What a silly place for this...How stupid to do that." Quietly Melric conjured up a wind to take them home for tea.

After tea the king sent for Melric. With the king was a painter called Vandee. "Melric," said the king, "I have had a brilliant idea. I have made Vandee the Royal mapmaker. Tomorrow and every day you will take him up in the balloon.

Each day he will paint part of the kingdom. I shall put the paintings side by side and have a huge picture map. Then I shall be able to plan all sorts of changes." "Straight roads are boring," Melric thought, "and some people like living close to their neighbours."

Melric didn't say anything. Instead he went for a ride in his balloon.

He wanted to think things over and so he just let the balloon...

...drift with the wind while he sat deep in thought.

Suddenly the balloon stopped with a bump.

"Watch where you are going, Melric," a voice said. Melric had hit the top of a mountain, not just any mountain but the mountain where Kra lived. Kra was a wise man who knew everything. He had helped Melric before when he had had problems. Now Kra said, "You must be careful when you interfere with other peoples' matters. Things are not always what they appear to be. Watch where you are going." "Thank you, Kra," said Melric, "I think I see what you mean." And with that Melric set off again while Kra slowly shook his head.

"Things are not always what they appear to be," repeated Melric. "And neither they will be," he murmured as he hurried off to the island where his cousin Guz the wizard lived. Guz was a helpful sort of chap who often changed the shape of his island just for fun, which was exactly what Melric wanted. Melric told Guz how the king wanted to change the kingdom and then he explained his plan to stop him. Every day Melric would guide the balloon to the island and every day Guz would make the island a different shape. Vandee would keep painting the same island thinking it was a different one. That way the map would never get finished and the king would forget about the changes. The next day Melric took Vandee to paint the island.

Every day the same thing happened; the magician and the mapmaker would set out early in the balloon. Melric steered the balloon different ways and at different speeds so that Vandee always thought they were going somewhere new.

But in fact they would always end up at the island. Of course it never looked the same thanks to Guz. Melric would just wait until Vandee had finished painting and then he would take them home again.

One evening, after another day of painting, Guz came to visit Melric. "How long is this going on?" Guz asked. "You sit up there wasting your time in the balloon every day while I and my pets have to stay hidden until you've gone. What are we going to do?"

Just then a messenger came to summon Melric to the king. "I'll try and tell him now," said Melric.

The king didn't look pleased. "I don't know what you're up to, Melric," he shouted, "but I do know we don't have as many islands as this. I want my map."

Then Melric burst out, "This is a lovely kingdom; the people are happy; they like you and they like the kingdom as it is and now you want to make changes. You'll spoil everything!"

The king was surprised. "I don't want to make changes," he said. "I only want to plan them. Sometimes it's more fun to plan things than to do them."

Melric groaned. "I've been a fool. Kra said things aren't always what they seem. Well then, here's your map," and with a flash he made the floor of the room look like the kingdom. "Now you can plan as much as you like."

"Come on, Guz," said Melric. "Vandee has his paintings; the king has his map; we need a rest. Let's go to your island, whatever shape it is."

"Good," said Guz, "but let's leave the balloon and go by magic. This time it will be more fun to arrive than to travel."

The Magician and the Crown

Melric, the magician, was going to visit Kra, the wise man who lived on a mountain.

'Make sure you're back for the ceremony of the crown,' said the King as Melric waved good-bye.

The ceremony of the crown happened once a year, when the King proved his right to rule by walking under a magical arch-shaped waterfall that tested his crown. If the crown was genuine, which of course it always was, a rainbow appeared and the crowd roared, 'Long live the King!'

After Melric had gone, the King played with his pet troon and watched the soldiers parade with their dragon mascot.

That evening the King enjoyed his bath but afterwards was annoyed to find that his crown was missing. 'It had better be here in the morning.' he said as the servants started to search.

In the morning the servants returned. The head servant started to speak: 'We can't find the . . .' and then he stopped and stared. The King was wearing the crown.

'It was there when I woke up,' said the King. 'I thought you'd returned it. Never mind. It was probably the troon playing tricks.'

Meanwhile, on the mountain, Kra was teaching Melric, his sister Mertel and Cousin Guz a spell that, used with water, let you see whatever you wanted.

'What would you like to see, Melric?' asked Kra.

'The King's crown, to remind me of the ceremony,' said Melric.

The pool became like a screen and there was the crown, but someone else was wearing it. 'Sondrak!' gasped Melric as he recognised his old enemy. 'What has happened to the King?'

The picture changed. There was the King, quite happy, also with a crown. 'I don't understand,' frowned Melric.

'You asked to see the crown. Sondrak has it,' said Kra. 'He is living with the gnomes, who are goldsmiths. They must have copied the crown to fool the King.'

'That's terrible,' said Melric. 'The King will fail the test and Sondrak will become King. I must do something.'

As Melric made a spell to take him back to the castle, Kra said, 'Remember, Melric, what's been done once can be done twice.'

Melric timed his return so that he arrived just after the King went for his bath. No sooner had he arrived than he left again, with the crown.

The King couldn't believe it when he saw the crown was missing again. He searched for it in vain. 'Now where have you put it?' he said to the troon.

While the King searched, Melric was hiding near where the gnomes lived, taking care not to be seen as they returned home for the night.

Once everything was quiet, Melric used Kra's spell on a water barrel to see Sondrak. There he was with the gnomes, wearing the crown and ordering them in a kingly voice to get firewood.

The firewood was near Melric. Quickly he put a spell on the wood and then hid as the gnomes came to collect it.

As the wood burned Melric's spell started to work. The fire gave off a pleasant smell that soon sent Sondrak and the gnomes into a wonderfully happy, dreamy sleep.

Once they were asleep, Melric went into the room and exchanged one crown for the other. Then, carrying the real crown, he returned to the castle.

In the morning the King was making a terrible commotion.

'What's all the fuss about?' asked Melric.

'Thank goodness you're back,' said the King. 'The troon is playing silly tricks with the crown, just to worry me. You'd better look after him until after the ceremony.'

The next day the ceremony started in the usual way. The King led a procession to the waterfall, where the people were waiting. But as he approached the waterfall there was a sudden shout, 'Behold the crown!' and Sondrak, wearing a crown, appeared from the rocks on the other side. The crowd gasped in astonishment. Then Sondrak said,

'I am your King.
To me you'll bow down
when you see proof
by test of the crown.'

Sondrak stepped under the waterfall and waited for the rainbow. It never came. Instead, the waterfall changed shape. The water stopped being an arch and fell straight on Sondrak, sending him into the lake below. The crowd chanted, 'Imposter. Imposter. Imposter,' and laughed at the sorcerer as he crawled out of the water. If there was one thing Sondrak couldn't stand it was being laughed at.

Melric explained everything to the King. 'Now I understand the disappearing crown,' said the King. 'If it hadn't been for you, Melric, that would be me in the water, and Sondrak would be King.' Then he called out,

'I am your King
and I'll do my best
to serve, if the crown
passes the test.'

He stood under the water, which had become an arch again, and the rainbow appeared. 'Long live the King!' roared the crowd.

Melric watched Sondrak as he slipped away. 'We fooled him again,' thought Melric. 'I wonder what he'll try next?'

The Magician's Apprentice

'Melric,' said King Jon to his magician, 'where is that young magician you're training for King Ralfe?'

'Rydar, my apprentice?' said Melric. 'Here he comes now. He's been away to learn from my cousin Guz and my sister Mertel.'

'Good,' said the King. 'Now I know you'd like more time to train Rydar but I don't like to think of my friend without a magician. Rydar can learn the rest later. We'll take him to King Ralfe tomorrow.'

100

The next morning they set off for King Ralfe's palace. Rydar was happy but Melric, who was still trying to teach him as they rode along, frowned. 'I wish I had time to teach you more,' he said. 'What did you learn from Guz and Mertel?'

'Guz showed me how to change things. You know how he loves to change his island,' laughed Rydar. 'Mertel taught me how to use a mirror. I'll show you when we stop.'

When they stopped for lunch Melric and Rydar walked to stretch their legs. Rydar took a mirror from his pocket.

'Good,' said Melric, 'so now you know reflection protection and through reflection, detection.' Then he stared.

In the mirror they could see Kra the wise man who had often helped Melric. 'Melric,' said Kra, 'take care. King Ralfe is a prisoner of your old enemy Sondrak. Now you will have to prove yourself, Rydar. I advise you that it is enough to do what you can do well.'

Kra disappeared as the King was calling, 'Come on, Melric, or we'll never get there.'

'Your Majesty, Rydar and I are going on alone. King Ralfe is in the power of Sondrak the Sorcerer. Return to the castle. When all is safe we will send for you.' Not giving the King time to speak Melric made a spell and he and Rydar disappeared.

The magician and his apprentice reappeared close to the palace of King Ralfe. Another spell, and they looked quite different. 'Now I'm a locksmith, but you're still my apprentice so you carry the tools,' smiled Melric. Rydar laughed. 'You may find this exciting,' said Melric, 'but take care. Sondrak is clever and evil.'

In the streets around the palace Melric shouted for work like the other craftsmen, 'Locks to mend?' They came to the palace door and waited until the captain of the guard arrived with a key. Melric made a quiet spell and the lock jammed. 'May I help you, Captain?' said Melric, stepping forward, and in no time he had the door open. 'If all the locks are like this one,' said Melric pretending to examine the lock, 'I'd better check them all. It would be awful if the King was locked in the bathroom.'

'Lucky you came along,' said the guard as Melric went inside.

Inside the castle Melric went straight to the King's adviser, whom he knew well. He explained his disguise and introduced Rydar.

'Sondrak has the King locked away,' explained the adviser. 'There is nothing we can do.'

'I have a plan,' said Melric, 'but we need your help to make it work.'

Melric went to search for the King, pretending to check the locks as he went. Then out of the corner of his eye he saw a dark figure approaching. 'What are you doing?' boomed a voice. Melric turned, his face bowed toward the ground. 'The captain said check all the locks, Your Majesty,' he croaked.

'Get on with it then,' said the man, looking pleased as he strode away.

'Your Majesty?' gasped Rydar in surprise.

'Sondrak,' whispered Melric. 'I was afraid he would recognise me. Come on.'

Quietly they followed Sondrak to a heavy door. He unlocked it and entered. Rydar held up his mirror so that the door was reflected. Then, looking through the reflection, they could see Sondrak talking to King Ralfe.

'Are you ready to march your army against King Jon and his stupid magician Melric?' said Sondrak.

'Never,' said King Ralfe. 'King Jon is my friend. He'll come to rescue me.'

'Stop dreaming,' snarled Sondrak. 'Do what I say. When I have Melric's kingdom, you'll have yours back. Think about it.'

Melric and Rydar hid while Sondrak left. When Sondrak had gone they changed back into their own clothes and went in to meet the King.

The King knew Melric and was delighted to see him. Melric introduced Rydar who said, 'Your Majesty, if I am to be your magician this has to be a job for me.'

'What can an apprentice do against Sondrak?' sighed the King.

'Rydar will do what he can do well,' said Melric, 'and Sondrak may be less careful against him. We have already thought out a plan. Now let's look for Sondrak,' he added and Rydar put his mirror where they could all see it.

They saw Sondrak quite clearly in the mirror. 'He's coming this way,' said King Ralfe.

'Time to confuse him,' said Melric. 'What's the room next to this one?'

'The library,' answered the King.

'Kitchen,' grinned Rydar and they watched Sondrak's look of surprise as he walked into the kitchen instead of the library. When he went back the way he had come he found himself in a games room, and so it went on. Rydar kept changing the palace around until Sondrak became completely lost. The adviser had warned the people of the palace, so they acted as if everything was normal. That confused Sondrak even more.

'We're ready for the next stage,' said Melric while the King laughed at Sondrak's antics. Another spell from Rydar, and Sondrak fell out onto the road.

'Now we have to go outside for the last act,' said Melric. 'You know what you have to do, Rydar. Off you go – good luck!' While Melric, Rydar and King Ralfe hurried on their way, Sondrak wandered about trying to work out where he was.

The King's adviser had warned everyone in the town as well as the palace what to expect. Now a long line of excited people trailed behind Sondrak, a very confused sorcerer.

Sondrak found himself in an open square. There, standing alone in the centre, was Rydar. The people lined the square to watch.

'Sondrak,' called Rydar, 'I am Rydar, the King's new magician. It is time for you to leave.'

'Now is the dangerous part,' said Melric to the King from where they watched.

'Magician? Ha!' laughed Sondrak, full of confidence. 'You're just a jumped-up boy. In fact I think you should jump some more. You can be a frog for a month. Then you'll have time to think.' Casually he flashed a spell at Rydar.

Rydar was ready and quickly held up his mirror so that the spell was reflected back to Sondrak.

'Ah! Yah! Groink! Groink!' croaked Sondrak as he changed into a frog.

Rydar quickly picked up the frog before it could escape. As the crowd strolled away Rydar gave the frog to a messenger. 'Take him to a pond as far from here as you can,' smiled Rydar. 'Perhaps we won't be troubled again for a while.'

'I'm proud to have you as my magician,' said King Ralfe. 'Now if you'll put everything back to normal we can send for King Jon and celebrate.'

'I'm proud of you too,' said Melric. 'One day you'll be a truly great magician, but be careful. We've stopped Sondrak for a while, but I'm sure we haven't heard the last of him.'